MW01242401

Copyright © 2022 By LaTeisha Patterson

Published and Printed in the United States

Cover and Book Design by LaTeisha Patterson

ISBN: 9798352219164

Table of Contents

Preface

In this season God is whispering in the wind to the watchman to get into position. Spiritual warfare is at an all time high. God's people must be alerted and intercession must be made.

This instruction and history of the Watchman will help to cultivate what is needed. Do not fear because the Lord our God Jesus Christ is with us.

Joshua 1:9 NIV *Have I not commanded you? Be strong and courageous. Do not be afraid; do not be discouraged, for the LORD your God will be with you wherever you go."*

A Word of Prayer

Father in the name of Jesus. I come before you to give thanks. Giving you all the praise and the honor. I repent of any sins known and unknown. I ask that you create in us a clean heart and renew a right spirit within us to do your will.

Lord God, I pray for the reader of this book that they may get the spirit of the word. I pray that they will have an ear to hear what you are saying. I bind and rebuke all distractions and confusion. Your word will perform the perfect will of what it was sent out to do. In Jesus name amen!

The Watchman

Ezekiel 3:17 "Son of man, I have made you a watchman for the people of Israel; so, hear the word I speak and give them warning from me.

What is a Watchman? The definition of a watchman is a person who keeps watch or guard. A watchman could also be called a custodian, guardian, keeper, lookout, warden or watcher.

The spiritual meaning of Watchman is someone who oversees what God has assigned them to. It could be a territory, people or an assigned word. The watchman brings the prophetic word to God's people. The watchman will also intercede on behalf of God's people because he has shown them what is to come.

What are the attributes of a Watchman?

Obedient: The word of God says in **Jeremiah 7:23 NIV** *but I gave them this command: Obey me, and I will be your God and you will be my people. Walk in obedience to all I command you, that it may go well with you.*

God also stated in **Deuteronomy 30:10 NIV** *if you obey the Lord your God and keep his commands and decrees that are written in this Book of the Law and turn to the Lord your God with all your heart and with all your soul.*

God is showing us that in our obedience is a blessing of safety and right standing with him.

An Ear to Hear in the Spirit: The word of God says in **1 Corinthians 2:14 ESV** *The natural person does not accept the things of the Spirit of God, for they are folly to him, and he is not able to understand them because they are spiritually discerned.* We cannot walk in carnality in our spiritual walk. We will not be able to clearly hear God's instruction.

This comes by the renewing of your mind on the daily. We find this instruction in **Romans 12:2 NIV** *Do not conform to the pattern of this world, but be transformed by the renewing of your mind. Then you will be able to test and approve what God's will is—his good, pleasing and perfect will.*

An Eye to See: **Matthew 13:16 AMP** says *but blessed [spiritually aware, and favored by God] are your eyes, because they see; and your ears, because they hear. ¹⁷ I assure you and most solemnly say to you, many prophets and righteous men [who were honorable and in right standing with God] longed to see what you see, and did not see it, and to hear what you hear, and did not hear it.*

Free of people's opinions: Being called to bring a word from God might bring an unfavorable opinion from others. But the key word is Called! God prepared you for the task at hand. The word of God says in **Romans 8:29-31 NIV** *For those God foreknew he also predestined to be conformed to the image of his Son, that he might be the firstborn among many brothers and sisters. ³⁰ And those he predestined, he also called; those he called, he also justified; those he justified, he also glorified. What, then, shall we say in response to these things? If God is for us, who can be against us?* Let this give you confidence in knowing the only opinion that matters is Gods.

A person of Strength and Courage: **Psalm 18:2-3 NIV** says *The Lord is my rock, my fortress and my deliverer; my God is my rock, in whom I take refuge, my shield and the horn of my salvation, my stronghold. ³ I called to the Lord, who is worthy of praise, and I have been saved from my enemies.* God is the source of strength and courage. He will provide any and everything that we need for the journey.

Love: **1 Corinthians 13:1-3 NIV** says *If I speak in the tongues of men or of angels, but do not have love, I am only a resounding gong or a clanging cymbal. ² If I have the gift of prophecy and can fathom all mysteries and all knowledge, and if I have a faith that can move mountains, but do not have love, I am nothing. ³ If I give all I possess to the poor and give over my body to hardship that I may boast but do not have love, I gain nothing.* We must love and have a heart for God's people as he has commanded.

These are just a few of the attributes that the Holy Spirit has shared with me. You might be thinking that you lack some of them. But just know that God will give you what you need according to his will and purpose.

If you feel you have all of these, humble yourself and ask God to examine your heart to see. Allow him to speak into you and give you what you need.

I want to discuss two watchmen that were called and the text that explains a part of their journey. We will be taking a look at Ezekiel and Daniel.

Ezekiel

Who is Ezekiel? Ezekiel was a God ordained prophet for the people of Israel. His name means God Strengthens. He served as a temple priest.
Ezekiel was called by God to deliver a message to the people of Israel.

We are going to take a deeper dive into the text in chapter 3 while Ezekiel saw a vision God had given him.

Ezekiel 3 NIV reads: *And he said to me, "Son of man, eat what is before you, eat this scroll; then go and speak to the people of Israel." ² So I opened my mouth, and he gave me the scroll to eat.*

³ Then he said to me, "Son of man, eat this scroll I am giving you and fill your stomach with it." So I ate it, and it tasted as sweet as honey in my mouth.

⁴ He then said to me: "Son of man, go now to the people of Israel and speak my words to them. *⁵ You are not being sent to a people of obscure speech and strange language, but to the people of Israel— ⁶ not to many peoples of obscure speech and strange language, whose words you cannot understand. Surely if I had sent you to them, they would have listened to you. ⁷ But the people of Israel are not willing to listen to you because they are not willing to listen to me, for all the Israelites are hardened and obstinate. ⁸ But I will make you as unyielding and hardened as they are. ⁹ I will make your forehead like the hardest stone, harder than flint. Do not be afraid of them or terrified by them, though they are a rebellious people."*

¹⁰ And he said to me, "Son of man, listen carefully and take to heart all the words I speak to you. ¹¹ Go now to your people in exile and speak to them. Say to them, 'This is what the Sovereign Lord says,' whether they listen or fail to listen."

¹² Then the Spirit lifted me up, and I heard behind me a loud rumbling sound as the glory of the Lord rose from the place where it was standing. ¹³ It was the sound of the wings of the living creatures brushing against each other and the sound of the wheels beside them, a loud rumbling sound. ¹⁴ The Spirit then lifted me up and took me away, and I went in bitterness and in the anger of my spirit, with the strong hand of the LORD on me. ¹⁵ I came to the exiles who lived at Tel Aviv near the Kebar River. And there, where they were living, I sat among them for seven days—deeply distressed.

Ezekiel's Task as Watchman

¹⁶ At the end of seven days the word of the LORD came to me: ¹⁷ "Son of man, I have made you a watchman for the people of Israel; so hear the word I speak and give them warning from me. ¹⁸ When I say to a wicked person, 'You will surely die,' and you do not warn them or speak out to dissuade them from their evil ways in order to save their life, that wicked person will die for their sin, and I will hold you accountable for their blood. ¹⁹ But if you do warn the wicked person and they do not turn from their wickedness or from their evil ways, they

will die for their sin; but you will have saved yourself.

20 *"Again, when a righteous person turns from their righteousness and does evil, and I put a stumbling block before them, they will die. Since you did not warn them, they will die for their sin. The righteous things that person did will not be remembered, and I will hold you accountable for their blood.* **21** *But if you do warn the righteous person not to sin and they do not sin, they will surely live because they took warning, and you will have saved yourself."*

22 *The hand of the L*ORD *was on me there, and he said to me, "Get up and go out to the plain, and there I will speak to you."* **23** *So I got up and went out to the plain. And the glory of the L*ORD *was standing there, like the glory I had seen by the Kebar River, and I fell facedown.*

24 *Then the Spirit came into me and raised me to my feet. He spoke to me and said: "Go, shut yourself inside your house.* **25** *And you, son of man, they will tie with ropes; you will be bound so that you cannot go out among the people.* **26** *I* *will make your tongue stick to the roof of your mouth so that you will be silent and unable to rebuke them, for they are a rebellious people. ²⁷ But when I speak to you, I will open your mouth and you shall say to them, 'This is what the Sovereign LORD says.' Whoever will listen let them listen, and whoever will refuse let them refuse; for they are a rebellious people.*

We can see in the text that God placed Ezekiel into a vision spiritually. If Ezekiel had been walking in carnality, he would have not been able to transition to the spirit realm for this message.

Romans 8:5-8 NIV says *Those who live according to the flesh have their minds set on what the flesh desires; but those who live in accordance with the Spirit have their minds set on what the Spirit desires. ⁶ The mind governed by the flesh is death, but the mind governed by the Spirit is life and peace. ⁷ The mind governed by the flesh is hostile to God; it does not submit to God's law, nor can it do so. ⁸ Those who are in the realm of the flesh cannot please God.*

We must try our best to stay in that sacred place with God. We never know when he is going to speak with us or give us a vision. The text further goes on to explain that God placed his words in Ezekiel's mouth and his message in his belly. The word of God was sweet to the taste for the man of God to carry even though it was a warning.

The Lord prepared Ezekiel for his journey and gave him tough skin to combat any backlash. He told Ezekiel his purpose and who he was (a Watchman). He told him to take on courage and not to be afraid because he was with him.

He was sent out to his own people so that they might understand him. So that there would be no confusion. God will not put you in a situation where you will not be received. It's up to the person to take heed to his message.

The people of Israel were very rebellious and refused to listen to the Lord and he let Ezekiel know what he was up against. But we can see in the text how God equipped him with everything he needed in order to give the message he had given him.

The word of God states whether they listen or not to give them the message. If we are not obedient in the calling the blood of those people is on our hands. If we give the message in obedience, we have saved ourselves. Verses 18-21 explains this very thing.

As Watchmen we love people and have compassion. As you can see, we can be sent to our own people. It may seem like a hard task to give what the Lord has said. But obedience is better than sacrifice. God is who you should revere and not man.

At the end of chapter 3 and in chapter 4 we see that God gave Ezekiel specific instruction on symbolic Illustration and intercession for the people of Israel and Judah.

(**Ezekiel 4 NIV** *"Now, son of man, take a block of clay, put it in front of you and draw the city of Jerusalem on it. ² Then lay siege to it: Erect siege works against it, build a ramp up to it, set up camps against it and put battering rams around it. ³ Then take an iron pan, place it as an iron wall between you and the city and turn your face toward it. It will be under siege, and you shall besiege it. This will be a sign to the people of Israel.*

⁴ "Then lie on your left side and put the sin of the people of Israel upon yourself. You are to bear their sin for the number of days you lie on your side. ⁵ I have assigned you the same number of days as the years of their sin. So for 390 days you will bear the sin of the people of Israel.

⁶ "After you have finished this, lie down again, this time on your right side, and bear the sin of the people of Judah. I have assigned you 40 days, a day for each year. ⁷ Turn your face toward the siege of Jerusalem and with bared arm prophesy against her. ⁸ I will tie you up with ropes so that you cannot turn from one side to the other until you have finished the days of your siege.

⁹ *"Take wheat and barley, beans and lentils, millet and spelt; put them in a storage jar and use them to make bread for yourself. You are to eat it during the 390 days you lie on your side.* ¹⁰ *Weigh out twenty shekels[b] of food to eat each day and eat it at set times.* ¹¹ *Also measure out a sixth of a hin of water and drink it at set times.* ¹² *Eat the food as you would a loaf of barley bread; bake it in the sight of the people, using human excrement for fuel."* ¹³ *The LORD said, "In this way the people of Israel will eat defiled food among the nations where I will drive them."*

¹⁴ *Then I said, "Not so, Sovereign LORD! I have never defiled myself. From my youth until now I have never eaten anything found dead or torn by wild animals. No impure meat has ever entered my mouth."*

¹⁵ *"Very well," he said, "I will let you bake your bread over cow dung instead of human excrement."*

¹⁶ He then said to me: "Son of man, I am about to cut off the food supply in Jerusalem. The people will eat rationed food in anxiety and drink rationed water in despair, ¹⁷ for food and water will be scarce. They will be appalled at the sight of each other and will waste away because of their sin.)

Ezekiel within this illustration and time of intercession was bearing the sins of the people. God gave him specific instruction on his meals and even compromised with him on the meals and how to cook it.

God is so awesome and what concerns us concerns him. God has had me standing in a stance of repentance for his people during prayer. So, sometimes we may be called to a demonstration in addition to our prayers.

We must realize as we move in the natural to do as we are called things are changing in the spirit. If Ezekiel had not been obedient to the Lord and done as instructed the people of Israel and Judah's blood would have been upon his hands.

Ezekiel was so selfless and obedient that he loved God and his people so much he did as instructed. I know this was not an easy task on the body naturally. You read further into Chapter 5 and see the entirety of what was required of him. Yet the Lord equipped him to do it.

As a watchman you will be on post day and night to blow the trumpet and carry the warning. If we do not blow that trumpet (give the warning) the blood is on our hands. Once we give the warning and the people do not take heed, they stand the consequence.

We find this to be true instruction in **Ezekiel 33:1-5 NIV** *The word of the LORD came to me:* *²* *"Son of man, speak to your people and say to them: 'When I bring the sword against a land, and the people of the land choose one of their men and make him their watchman,* *³* *and he sees the sword coming against the land and blows the trumpet to warn the people,* *⁴* *then if anyone hears the trumpet but does not heed the warning and the sword comes and takes their life, their blood will be on their own head.* *⁵* *Since* *they heard the sound of the trumpet but did not heed the warning, their blood will be on their own head.*

If they had heeded the warning, they would have saved themselves. ⁶ But if the watchman sees the sword coming and does not blow the trumpet to warn the people and the sword comes and takes someone's life, that person's life will be taken because of their sin, but I will hold the watchman accountable for their blood.'

Daniel

Who is Daniel? Daniel was a prophet under the rule of Nebuchadnezzar. He was a man of strong faith and courage. He is most known for being thrown in the fiery furnace and came out unscathed because God was with him. Daniel's name means God is my judge.

Daniel was a watchman in the kingdom he served. He would interpret dreams for the king and it made him a believer of God. Daniel's obedience to God shows a wayward king who the one and true living God was. We are going to take a look at **Daniel 10**.

In the third year of Cyrus king of Persia, a revelation was given to Daniel (who was called Belteshazzar). Its message was true and it concerned a great war. The understanding of the message came to him in a vision.

² At that time I, Daniel, mourned for three weeks. ³ I ate no choice food; no meat or wine touched my lips; and I used no lotions at all until the three weeks were over.

4 On the twenty-fourth day of the first month, as I was standing on the bank of the great river, the Tigris, **5** I looked up and there before me was a man dressed in linen, with a belt of fine gold from Uphaz around his waist. **6** His body was like topaz, his face like lightning, his eyes like flaming torches, his arms and legs like the gleam of burnished bronze, and his voice like the sound of a multitude.

7 I, Daniel, was the only one who saw the vision; those who were with me did not see it, but such terror overwhelmed them that they fled and hid themselves. **8** So I was left alone, gazing at this great vision; I had no strength left, my face turned deathly pale and I was helpless. **9** Then I heard him speaking, and as I listened to him, I fell into a deep sleep, my face to the ground.

10 A hand touched me and set me trembling on my hands and knees. **11** He said, "Daniel, you who are highly esteemed, consider carefully the words I am about to speak to you, and stand up, for I have now been sent to you." And when he said this to me, I stood up trembling.

¹² Then he continued, "Do not be afraid, Daniel. Since the first day that you set your mind to gain understanding and to humble yourself before your God, your words were heard, and I have come in response to them. ¹³ But the prince of the Persian kingdom resisted me twenty-one days. Then Michael, one of the chief princes, came to help me, because I was detained there with the king of Persia. ¹⁴ Now I have come to explain to you what will happen to your people in the future, for the vision concerns a time yet to come."

¹⁵ While he was saying this to me, I bowed with my face toward the ground and was speechless. ¹⁶ Then one who looked like a man touched my lips, and I opened my mouth and began to speak. I said to the one standing before me, "I am overcome with anguish because of the vision, my lord, and I feel very weak. ¹⁷ How can I, your servant, talk with you, my lord? My strength is gone and I can hardly breathe."

18 Again the one who looked like a man touched me and gave me strength. 19 "Do not be afraid, you who are highly esteemed," he said. "Peace! Be strong now; be strong."

When he spoke to me, I was strengthened and said, "Speak, my lord, since you have given me strength."

20 So he said, "Do you know why I have come to you? Soon I will return to fight against the prince of Persia, and when I go, the prince of Greece will come; 21 but first I will tell you what is written in the Book of Truth. No one supports me against them except Michael, your prince.

Daniel, being a man of faith, had been in mourning and fasting for 3 weeks (21 days) because of a great war that was to come. God honored Daniel and his prayers so much that he answered at the very moment he sought God to get understanding.

The enemy however was on watch as well began spiritual opposition. At times we are called to fast and pray for an answer. God answered that prayer as soon as we asked him. This scripture is proof of that.

As a watchman, prophet and intercessor you will get opposition. But God! The word says in Isaiah 59:19 KJV *So shall they fear the name of the LORD from the west, and his glory from the rising of the sun. When the enemy shall come in like a flood, the Spirit of the LORD shall lift up a standard against him.* God sends us help, we just have to hold on and stay in the process. That is what he did for Daniel.

When we feel weak, God will strengthen us. **2 Corinthians 12:10 NIV** says *Therefore I take pleasure in infirmities, in reproaches, in necessities, in persecutions, in distresses for Christ's sake: for when I am weak, then am I strong.*

Daniel felt weak in the presence of the messenger but he spoke a word of strength back into him. Once again God equipped him for the word and journey.

Can you imagine fasting and no self-care for three weeks as a demonstration of intercession for your people? I can only imagine how weak his natural body was in that process. But he held on because he knew that God would come and give him his answer. What a man of faith which is pleasing to the Lord.

Hebrews 11:6 NIV says *and **without faith** it is impossible to please God, because anyone who comes to him must believe that he exists and that he rewards those who earnestly seek him.*

With this vision of the messenger Daniel was the only one who had the eye to see and ear to hear. The people around him felt the glory of God and fled. The people around you may feel God's glory but they do not have the anointing and calling on their life to see and hear the message.

When we get the message it's important to ask God when it's the right time to release it. At the appointed time the people will receive and understand what the spirit of the Lord is saying. That is if they are connected in the spirit.

Carnal minded people will not understand the word of God or warning. The natural thing to do is try to analyze and find a significant meaning of the word within our own selves. But that is not what God has called us to do.

1 Corinthians 1:27 NIV says *But God chose the foolish things of the world to shame the wise; God chose the weak things of the world to shame the strong.* The word of God is foolishness to the word. He that has an ear let him hear what the spirit of the Lord is saying to his people and heed his warnings.

The word of God has called us to pray for understanding and wisdom. You must have faith to believe that you will receive it. **Proverbs 4:7 NIV** says *the beginning of wisdom is this: Get Wisdom. Though it cost all you have, get understanding.*

James 1:5-8 NIV says *If any of you lacks wisdom, you should ask God, who gives generously to all without finding fault, and it will be given to you. ⁶ But when you ask, you must believe and not doubt, because the one who doubts is like a* wave of the sea, blown and tossed by the wind. *7 That person should not expect to receive anything from the Lord. *8 Such a person is double-minded and unstable in all they do.*

We see from these two examples of watchmen in the word of God that we have to be consecrated to receive the message from God.

Romans 12:1-2 NIV says *Therefore, I urge you, brothers and sisters, in view of God's mercy, to offer your bodies as a living sacrifice, holy and pleasing to God—this is your true and proper worship. *2 Do not conform to the pattern of this world, but be transformed by the renewing of your mind. Then you will be able to test and approve what God's will is—his good, pleasing and perfect will.*

To carry the word, we must be well equipped. **Ephesians 6:10-17 NIV** says *Finally, be strong in the Lord and in his mighty power. *11 Put on the full armor of God, so that you can take your stand against the devil's schemes. *12 For our struggle is not against flesh and blood, but against the rulers, against the* *authorities, against the powers of this dark world and against the spiritual forces of evil in the heavenly realms.* **¹³** *Therefore put on the full armor of God, so that when the day of evil comes, you may be able to stand your ground, and after you have done everything, to stand.* **¹⁴** *Stand firm then, with the belt of truth buckled around your waist, with the breastplate of righteousness in place,* **¹⁵** *and with your feet fitted with the readiness that comes from the gospel of peace.* **¹⁶** *In addition to all this, take up the shield of faith, with which you can extinguish all the flaming arrows of the evil one.* **¹⁷** *Take the helmet of salvation and the sword of the Spirit, which is the word of God.*

We must keep in mind who the real enemy is while performing our calling. We might be backlash and push back from the people but the true enemy is the devil and his workers.

 Ephesians 6:12 NIV says *for our struggle is not against flesh and blood, but against the rulers, against the authorities, against the powers of this dark world and against the spiritual forces of evil in the heavenly realms.*

Remember that you must always be on watch for the enemy and remain in prayer. When you pray, use your heavenly language. **Ephesians 6:18 NIV** *And pray in the Spirit on all occasions with all kinds of prayers and requests. With this in mind, be alert and always keep on praying for all the Lord's people.*

Stand in your Purpose and Authority

God placed the Watchmen in place to disrupt the enemies plans in the spirit realm. God gave us the ability to intercept the attacks with beforehand knowledge. By way of our obedience to God's direct instructions.

Watchmen have the ability of foresight by way of the Holy Spirit. We must wake up and stay in position to make preparation to ward off attacks and warn God's people. Sound the alarm when God gives you the signal. Stand at arms equipped with the Holy Spirit and God's word which is your weapon.

The word of God says in **Luke 10:19 NIV**, *I have given you authority to trample on snakes and scorpions and to overcome all the power of the enemy; nothing will harm you.* Do not allow fear to overtake you during the battle.

2 Timothy 1:7 AMP says *For God did not give us a spirit of timidity or cowardice or fear, but [He has given us a spirit] of power and of love and of*

*sound judgment and personal discipline
[abilities that result in a calm, well-balanced
mind and self-control].*

Open your mouth and proclaim the word that
the Lord has given you for his purpose and plan.
Be used as a vessel for his glory. The word of
God cuts sharper than any double-edged sword.

Hebrews 4:12 AMP says *for the word of God is
living and active and full of power [making it
operative, energizing, and effective]. It is
sharper than any two-edged sword, penetrating
as far as the division of the soul and spirit [the
completeness of a person], and of both joints
and marrow [the deepest parts of our nature],
exposing and judging the very thoughts and
intentions of the heart.*
When we speak under the unction of the Holy
Spirit it penetrates the atmosphere. Things
begin to shift first spiritually and then manifest
in the natural. Know who you are and work
within your calling and purpose.

Scriptures on Authority

Matthew 16:19 AMP *I will give you the keys (authority) of the kingdom of heaven; and whatever you bind [forbid, declare to be improper and unlawful] on earth will have [already] been bound in heaven, and whatever you loose [permit, declare lawful] on earth will have [already] been loosed in heaven."*

John 14:12 AMP *I assure you and most solemnly say to you, anyone who believes in Me [as Savior] will also do the things that I do; and he will do even greater things than these [in extent and outreach], because I am going to the Father.*

Matthew 28:18-20 AMP *Jesus came up and said to them, "All authority (all power of absolute rule) in heaven and on earth has been given to Me. [19] Go therefore and make disciples of all the nations [help the people to learn of Me, believe in Me, and obey My words], baptizing them in the name of the Father and of the Son and of the Holy*

Spirit, [20] *teaching them to observe everything that I have commanded you; and lo, I am with you always [remaining with you perpetually— regardless of circumstance, and on every occasion], even to the end of the age."*

Psalm 91:13 AMP *You will tread upon the lion and cobra; The young lion and the serpent you will trample underfoot.*

James 4:7 AMP *So submit to [the authority of] God. Resist the devil [stand firm against him] and he will flee from you.*

1 John 4:4 *Little children (believers, dear ones), you are of God and you belong to Him and have [already] overcome them [the agents of the antichrist]; because He who is in you is greater than he (Satan) who is in the world [of sinful mankind].*

Scriptures on Purpose

1 Peter 2:9 NIV *But you are a chosen people, a royal priesthood, a holy nation, God's special possession, that you may declare the praises of him who called you out of darkness into his wonderful light.*

Colossians 1:16 NIV *For in him all things were created: things in heaven and on earth, visible and invisible, whether thrones or powers or rulers or authorities; all things have been created through him and for him.*

Jeremiah 29:11 NIV *For I know the plans I have for you," declares the LORD, "plans to prosper you and not to harm you, plans to give you hope and a future.*

Romans 8:28 NIV *And we know that in all things God works for the good of those who love him, who have been called according to his purpose.*

Ephesians 2:10 NIV *For we are God's handiwork, created in Christ Jesus to do good works, which God prepared in advance for us to do.*

Philippians 2:13 NIV *for it is God who works in you to will and to act in order to fulfill his good purpose.*

Ephesians 1:11 NIV *In him we were also chosen, having been predestined according to the plan of him who works out everything in conformity with the purpose of his will.*

Isaiah 55:10-11 NIV *As the rain and the snow come down from heaven, and do not return to it without watering the earth and making it bud and flourish, so that it yields seed for the sower and bread for the eater, 11 so is my word that goes out from my mouth: It will not return to me empty, but will accomplish what I desire and achieve the purpose for which I sent it.*

A Word of Prayer

Father God, I come before you humbly giving you all the praise, glory and honor. I thank you for allowing your word to go forth by way of me being a willing vessel.

I pray that these words penetrate the atmosphere and perform what you have set out for it to do. I thank you in advance for the manifestation of your glory, purpose and plan for your people.

I thank you that the reader will have a fire ignited within their spirit and be encouraged to launch out into the deep of your calling.

Your word says greater is he that is within me than he that is in the world. We thank you that you live within us guiding us with all power and authority. In Jesus name amen!

Made in the USA
Middletown, DE
06 October 2022

11733387R00022